Keys
A MANUAL FOR LIFE.
UPHOLD31:8

WELCOME! to Mental Health Keys

If you picked up this manual, I am guessing it is with the intention that you want to manage your Mental Health, more effectively. Mental Health Keys: The Manual is a guide to help you manage your mental health symptoms on a daily basis. It is a tool to help guide along this journey of life providing reassurance and accountability. Mental Health plays a role in everything we do, even if we do not see it. So why not utilize a tool that can help you manage it, reinforcing that you are monitoring your Mental Health, daily. Inside you will find positive affirmations, scriptures, quotes, monthly calendar, note page and word bank for mental health symptoms. Utilize these different pieces for added motivation, inspiration and spiritual guidance.

How to Best Use This Manual

Use the calendar to track your mental health symptoms daily. The word bank in the back of the manual will give you a collection of mental health symptoms that you can write in on the calendar. You have five lines to utilize in each day of the month, so take advantage! Feel free to create your own symptoms or jot down your feelings in addition. This gives you an accurate depiction of what your mental health looks like on a day-to- day basis, a monthly basis and yearly basis. If you are already in therapy or even if you see a medical doctor, you can provide proof of your symptoms!

Use the monthly recap page, to write out your wins, goals or anything else you are proud of for the month in Accomplishments. In the next box write in any upcoming projects, events, connections you are looking forward to doing under Opportunities.

Use the free space page to journal, draw, create, and doodle, wherever you feel inclined to do this what this space is for.

Thank you for purchasing and I hope this manual is helpful in maintaining your Mental Health!

Now that is a #MentalHealthKey

-Gary "Trey" Taylor

April

TRUST GOD

April 2018

Sun	Mon	Tue	Wed	Thu	Fri	Sat
1	2	3	4	5	6	7
8	9	10	11	12	13	14
15	16	17	18	19	20	21
22	23	24	25	26	27	28
29	30					

Rain is synonymous with many things. Some see it in the scientific ways, evaporated water stored up creating precipitation. You remember what they taught in science class right? Or now our new science reporting that we can control the weather, a topic for another day. Socially some see rain as a period of sadness, often correlated to depressive themes the blues or being down. I guess people correlate tears to rain drops, unsure why we do so. Growing up as a country boy I have learned to accept rainy days for peacefulness. I understand rain to be peaceful, a period of time to reflect, slow down and relax. A rainy day allows me to organize my thoughts, categorize and let go. The whole moniker "when it rains it pours" can present differently in this case.

Accomplishments

Opportunities

WHAT WE THINK AFFECTS
HOW WE ACT AND FEEL.

THOUGHT

EMOTION

BEHAVIOUR

WHAT WE FEEL AFFECTS
HOW WE THINK AND DO.

WHAT WE DO AFFECTS
HOW WE THINK AND FEEL.

Notes

FREE Space

WRITE. DRAW. CREATE.

May

KEEP THAT SAME ENERGY

May 2018

Sun	Mon	Tue	Wed	Thu	Fri	Sat
29	30	1	2	3	4	5
6	7	8	9	10	11	12
13	14	15	16	17	18	19
20	21	22	23	24	25	26
27	28	29	30	31		

The sound of a steady rain drop allows time to focus. With every drop there is a thought. With every thought there is a decision to make. Do I keep this thought, file it or let it go? I feel as if the rain is preparing me for the sunny and clear day. You know the beautiful day where everything is just right? What if that rain never comes and you never get a chance to sit and reflect, to organize your thoughts. Could it be that the rain in all its negative connotation is actually preparation or a natural reset in order for our next day of sunshine? You know since we correlate sunshine and sunny days to positivity and joy. Could it be that rain is actually positive and it's a self-cleaning mechanism mentally so that we can enjoy our beautiful days to the fullest.

Never neglect the rain, for the rain is the precursor to our joy.

MONTHLY *Recap*

Accomplishments

Opportunities

WHAT WE THINK AFFECTS
HOW WE ACT AND FEEL.

THOUGHT

EMOTION

BEHAVIOUR

WHAT WE FEEL AFFECTS
HOW WE THINK AND DO.

WHAT WE DO AFFECTS
HOW WE THINK AND FEEL.

Notes

FREE Space
WRITE. DRAW. CREATE.

UPHOLD 31:8

June

BE COMFORTABLE IN YOUR OWN SKIN

June 2018

Sun	Mon	Tue	Wed	Thu	Fri	Sat
27	28	29	30	31	1	2
3	4	5	6	7	8	9
10	11	12	13	14	15	16
17	18	19	20	21	22	23
24	25	26	27	28	29	30

What I've learned is that the mind is also a fine tuned machine, much like the human body. It has periods where it can be "hitting on all cylinders" but times where it's "lagging". This is where I think our mental health comes into play. There are times whether it be super late at night or during the day, evening, where the mind needs time to recharge and tune itself back up. The tune however is not only rooted in just sleep, or decompression. It's also found in a place of deep cognitive thought, processing the often racing thoughts of the day, slowed down to effectively address them or rid them of the mind. This mental tune up can be coupled with prayer, or meditation. Actually it should be. At this current moment, I'm not stressed out about anything. There is a sense of peace and just deep slow flowing thoughts. Anyways if you find yourself in this place, every once in a while, fret not, it seems to be natural and also necessary.

Accomplishments

Opportunities

WHAT WE THINK AFFECTS
HOW WE ACT AND FEEL.

THOUGHT

EMOTION

BEHAVIOUR

WHAT WE FEEL AFFECTS
HOW WE THINK AND DO.

WHAT WE DO AFFECTS
HOW WE THINK AND FEEL.

Notes

WRITE. DRAW. CREATE.

July

LET GO OF THINGS YOU CAN NOT CONTROL

July 2018

Sun	Mon	Tue	Wed	Thu	Fri	Sat
1	2	3	4	5	6	7
8	9	10	11	12	13	14
15	16	17	18	19	20	21
22	23	24	25	26	27	28
29	30	31				

I feel as if most creatives, millennials, or the working American in general have the same feelings and are just pushing through it. I am hear to tell you STOP, and figure out a plan to address it. We're so charged up ready to take on the world and attending to everyone else needs but ourselves. I know you heard it time and time again but I am telling you to STOP IT NOW. {SELF} meaning you can not be helpful to anyone if you can not be the best version of yourself everyday. Take time, no I mean take time for yourself. If that ain't you, take time to release from life, unplug rather give your mind a rest. This time throughout the day can have long-lasting effects outside of just doing your favorite hobby or exercising. Stress can lead to anxiety disorders, depression, medical conditions and physiological conditions including lack of sleep and appetite, irritability, mood swings and changes.

MONTHLY *Recap*

Accomplishments

Opportunities

WHAT WE THINK AFFECTS
HOW WE ACT AND FEEL.

THOUGHT

EMOTION

BEHAVIOUR

WHAT WE FEEL AFFECTS
HOW WE THINK AND DO.

WHAT WE DO AFFECTS
HOW WE THINK AND FEEL.

Notes

WRITE. DRAW. CREATE.

August

TRUST THE PROCESS

August 2018

Sun	Mon	Tue	Wed	Thu	Fri	Sat
29	30	31	1	2	3	4
5	6	7	8	9	10	11
12	13	14	15	16	17	18
19	20	21	22	23	24	25
26	27	28	29	30	31	

I feel as if most creatives, millennials, or the working American in general have the same feelings and are just pushing through it. I am hear to tell you STOP, and figure out a plan to address it. We're so charged up ready to take on the world and attending to everyone else needs but ourselves. I know you heard it time and time again but I am telling you to STOP IT NOW. {SELF} meaning you can not be helpful to anyone if you can not be the best version of yourself everyday. Take time, no I mean take time for yourself. If that ain't you, take time to release from life, unplug rather give your mind a rest. This time throughout the day can have long-lasting effects outside of just doing your favorite hobby or exercising. Stress can lead to anxiety disorders, depression, medical conditions and physiological conditions including lack of sleep and appetite, irritability, mood swings and changes.

Accomplishments

Opportunities

WHAT WE THINK AFFECTS
HOW WE ACT AND FEEL.

THOUGHT

EMOTION

BEHAVIOUR

WHAT WE FEEL AFFECTS
HOW WE THINK AND DO.

WHAT WE DO AFFECTS
HOW WE THINK AND FEEL.

Notes

WRITE. DRAW. CREATE.

September

THE GRIND DOES STOP. RE-CHARGE

September 2018

Sun	Mon	Tue	Wed	Thu	Fri	Sat
26	27	28	29	30	31	1
2	3	4	5	6	7	8
9	10	11	12	13	14	15
16	17	18	19	20	21	22
23	24	25	26	27	28	29
30	1	2	3	4	5	6

Stress can lead to chest pains. Come up with a plan to combat your stress, to assure you are doing all you can to do to be mentally, spiritually, and physically well and healthy! Somehow we neglect how much stress can affect us, we ignore it suppress it and it flares up in places we wouldn't think. Be mindful and take control of your stress, don't let stress control you.

MONTHLY *Recap*

Accomplishments

Opportunities

WHAT WE THINK AFFECTS
HOW WE ACT AND FEEL.

THOUGHT

EMOTION

BEHAVIOUR

WHAT WE FEEL AFFECTS
HOW WE THINK AND DO.

WHAT WE DO AFFECTS
HOW WE THINK AND FEEL.

Notes

WRITE. DRAW. CREATE.

October

YOU WERE CREATED FOR THIS MOMENT

October 2018

Sun	Mon	Tue	Wed	Thu	Fri	Sat
30	1	2	3	4	5	6
7	8	9	10	11	12	13
14	15	16	17	18	19	20
21	22	23	24	25	26	27
28	29	30	31			

Don't ever take for granted your failures and struggles in life. These are the things that shape and mold you into the person you will become in the near future. A 1.8 GPA can turn into a 2.7 with a Bachelor's degree, four years later that turns into a 3.7 and a Masters degree. It's not about how you perform during the battle, it's how you finish.

MONTHLY *Recap*

Accomplishments

Opportunities

WHAT WE THINK AFFECTS
HOW WE ACT AND FEEL.

THOUGHT

EMOTION

BEHAVIOUR

WHAT WE FEEL AFFECTS
HOW WE THINK AND DO.

WHAT WE DO AFFECTS
HOW WE THINK AND FEEL.

Notes

FREE Space

WRITE. DRAW. CREATE.

November

NOTHING GREAT IS CREATED OUT OF COMFORT

November 2018

Sun	Mon	Tue	Wed	Thu	Fri	Sat
29	30	30	31	1	2	3
4	5	6	7	8	9	10
11	12	13	14	15	16	17
18	19	20	21	22	23	24
25	26	27	28	29	30	

Never get complacent. Continue to learn and grow. Seek out new opportunities, and challenges. It will help aide in your mental health and help grow your business. Mental Health = how you deal with day to day life stressors.

MONTHLY *Recap*

Accomplishments

Opportunities

WHAT WE THINK AFFECTS
HOW WE ACT AND FEEL.

THOUGHT

EMOTION

BEHAVIOUR

WHAT WE FEEL AFFECTS
HOW WE THINK AND DO.

WHAT WE DO AFFECTS
HOW WE THINK AND FEEL.

Notes

FREE Space
WRITE. DRAW. CREATE.

UPHOLD 31:8

December

TRUST IN YOUR {SELF}

December 2018

Sun	Mon	Tue	Wed	Thu	Fri	Sat
25	26	27	28	29	30	1
2	3	4	5	6	7	8
9	10	11	12	13	14	15
16	17	18	19	20	21	22
23	24	25	26	27	28	29
30	31	1	2	3	4	5

Understand when you are the most productive and build your schedule around it. I find my greatest productivity is around 11am-1pm, and evenings around 5-7pm. The times where you are not most productive, should be times where you are taking a break and doing something to take your mind off work. The mind is not made to constantly work, work and work let alone stare at a computer screen for hours at a time. Think about how much the mind is subconsciously working without you knowing. Then add on your business. Take care of your mind, and it will take care of you.

Accomplishments

Opportunities

WHAT WE THINK AFFECTS
HOW WE ACT AND FEEL.

THOUGHT

EMOTION

BEHAVIOUR

WHAT WE FEEL AFFECTS
HOW WE THINK AND DO.

WHAT WE DO AFFECTS
HOW WE THINK AND FEEL.

Notes

WRITE. DRAW. CREATE.

January

BE THE CHANGE
YOU WANT TO SEE

January 2019

Sun	Mon	Tue	Wed	Thu	Fri	Sat
30	31	1	2	3	4	5
6	7	8	9	10	11	12
13	14	15	16	17	18	19
20	21	22	23	24	25	26
27	28	29	30	31		

Sleep, sleep, sleep. Be sure you are getting the adequate hours of sleep nightly. Most can function anywhere from 5-9 hours of sleep. You should know how many hours of sleeps equals productivity. I typically need 6 to 7 hours of solid sleep to be productive. I have heard of those who function off of 4-5 hours.

MONTHLY *Recap*

Accomplishments

Opportunities

WHAT WE THINK AFFECTS
HOW WE ACT AND FEEL.

THOUGHT

WHAT WE FEEL AFFECTS
HOW WE THINK AND DO.

EMOTION

BEHAVIOUR

WHAT WE DO AFFECTS
HOW WE THINK AND FEEL.

Notes

ÚPHOLD

WRITE. DRAW. CREATE.

February 2019

Sun	Mon	Tue	Wed	Thu	Fri	Sat
27	28	29	30	31	1	2
3	4	5	6	7	8	9
10	11	12	13	14	15	16
17	18	19	20	21	22	23
24	25	26	27	28		

When things do not go as planned or I feel as though I am being average I get frustrated because I know I am so much greater. Now here is the kicker, with trusting God and knowing who you are within Christ why settle for just normal? Yes be thankful for the blessings that you do have never ever take them for granted. God tells us that we are fearfully and wonderfully made, that we are the head and not the tail, above and not beneath, greater works that we will do. We are Eagles! And Eagles soar high! Why not try God for that crazy idea that you do not believe will happen. Why not believe you can own and operate your own business rather being stuck in that 9-5. Never succumb to the masses who tell you these things are not possible. The opinion of man is inferior to God. Step out on faith on whatever you are holding back on. You do not want to place limits on God whom is limitless. Good afternoon.

MONTHLY *Recap*

Accomplishments

Opportunities

WHAT WE THINK AFFECTS
HOW WE ACT AND FEEL.

THOUGHT

EMOTION

BEHAVIOUR

WHAT WE FEEL AFFECTS
HOW WE THINK AND DO.

WHAT WE DO AFFECTS
HOW WE THINK AND FEEL.

Notes

FREE *Space*

WRITE. DRAW. CREATE.

FOLLOW YOUR INSTINCT

March 2019

Sun	Mon	Tue	Wed	Thu	Fri	Sat
24	25	26	27	28	1	2
3	4	5	6	7	8	9
10	11	12	13	14	15	16
17	18	19	20	21	22	23
24	25	26	27	28	29	30
31	1	2	3	4	5	6

If your plate is full, and God did not ordain it, then it is time to clean your plate off. The burdens create panic and anxiety in our lives. The Bible says to worry is a sin. It also says Matthew 6:34 NKJV "Therefore do not worry about tomorrow, for tomorrow will worry about itself. Sufficient for today is its own trouble." God does not burden us, we burden ourselves, it's a choice why do we continue to do so?. God never wants you to be so busy, that you push him to the side. Yet that's what we usually do. Cast your burdens on the Lord, he will provide for you and make a way for the desires of your heart. Its time we let go and Let God

MONTHLY *Recap*

Accomplishments

Opportunities

WHAT WE THINK AFFECTS
HOW WE ACT AND FEEL.

THOUGHT

EMOTION

BEHAVIOUR

WHAT WE FEEL AFFECTS
HOW WE THINK AND DO.

WHAT WE DO AFFECTS
HOW WE THINK AND FEEL.

Notes

WRITE. DRAW. CREATE.

<h1 style="text-align:center">Word Bank</h1>

HAPPY	FLASHBACKS	AUDITORY HALLUCINATIONS
SAD	HEADACHES	VISUAL HALLUCINATIONS
OPTIMISTIC	MIGRAINES	DELUSIONS
HELPLESS	FATIGUE	PARANOIA
PEACEFUL	PANIC ATTACKS	SUICIDAL THOUGHTS
POOR SLEEP	RESTLESSNESS	HOMICIDAL THOUGHTS
IRRITABLE	OVER-THINKING	SUICIDAL PLANS
POOR APPETITE	HOPELESSNESS	SUICIDAL INTENT
POSITIVE	WORTHLESSNESS	HOMICIDAL PLANS
THANKFUL	SHORT OF BREATH	HOMICIDAL INTENT
ANXIOUS	CONFUSION	SELF-HARM
EUSTRESS	ANGER	CUTTING
DIFFICULTY CONCENTRATING	FRUSTRATION	PLANS TO CUT
EXCITED	ANXIETY	ALCOHOL ABUSE
DIFFICULT FOCUSING	DEPRESSED	SUBSTANCE ABUSE
HOPEFUL	STRESS	MARIJUANA ABUSE
RESILIENT	GRIEF	
WORRIED	ALCOHOL USE	
ENTHUSIASTIC	MIGRAINES	
ENERGETIC	RACING THOUGHTS	
	MARIJUANA USE	

<h1 style="text-align:center">Some More Space</h1>

FREE Space
WRITE. DRAW. CREATE.

UPHOLD 31:8

FREE *Space*

WRITE. DRAW. CREATE.

FREE *Space*

WRITE. DRAW. CREATE.